Original title:
Holding On to Me

Copyright © 2024 Swan Charm
All rights reserved.

Author: Aron Pilviste
ISBN HARDBACK: 978-9916-79-099-1
ISBN PAPERBACK: 978-9916-79-100-4
ISBN EBOOK: 978-9916-79-101-1

The Fabric of My Spirit

In whispers soft, the dawn unfolds,
A tapestry of dreams retold.
Each thread a hope, each color bright,
We weave our lives in morning light.

Through trials faced and joy embraced,
The fabric shifts, yet holds its grace.
With every tear, a new design,
In storms we grow, our roots entwine.

The laughter shared, the tears we shed,
A quilt of moments, softly spread.
In every stitch, a memory sewn,
A sacred place we call our own.

Each vibrant patch, our stories speak,
In silent strength, we find the weak.
Together strong, we brave the night,
Our spirits soar, as we take flight.

So as I stand, both brave and free,
I wear this fabric, part of me.
In every shade, I find my part,
A rich kaleidoscope of heart.

Threads of Identity

In every scar, a story we find,
Woven through time, both gentle and blind.
Colors of laughter, shades of our pain,
Together they dance, like sun through the rain.

Roots delve deeper, where memories grow,
Echoes of whispers, the tales that we know.
Branches reaching out, to touch and embrace,
In the tapestry's heart, we all find our place.

Nurturing the Unseen

In silence, we nurture the seeds yet to bloom,
Tending the dreams that reside in the gloom.
A whisper of hope on the lips of the night,
Allows the soft wishes to unfold into light.

The invisible bonds that intertwine our fate,
Carry us gently, through struggles and weight.
Each thought a petal, each feeling a sigh,
Collecting the moments as time dances by.

My Light Among the Stars

When darkness envelops the wide open sea,
I search for constellations that comfort me.
My light may be small, but it flickers so bright,
Guiding lost sailors through long, starry nights.

Each star is a promise, a dream yet to chase,
A mapping of journeys, each guiding grace.
In the vastness above, I find my own way,
My spirit connected, to night and to day.

The Reverie of Remembering

In the quiet moments, memories bloom,
Like flowers in spring, dispelling the gloom.
Echoes of laughter, whispers of love,
Drift softly like clouds in the skies above.

Through the veil of time, I wander and roam,
Finding the pieces that build me a home.
Each glance backward sparks a light so divine,
In the reverie of remembering, I align.

A Heart's Reflection

In the stillness of night,
My heart whispers soft light.
Memories dance like shadows,
Lost in time's gentle flows.

A mirror of my soul,
Pieces that make me whole.
Echoes of laughter bright,
Fading into the night.

Choices that I have made,
In sunlight and in shade.
Each moment crystal clear,
Reflections drawing near.

A tender touch of grace,
A bittersweet embrace.
Hold tight what must be free,
In my heart's tapestry.

Within a silent sigh,
I learn to say goodbye.
In the depths of my soul,
A heart's reflection—whole.

The Weight of Forgotten Dreams

Whispers of what could be,
Frayed at the edges, free.
Shattered hopes lost in time,
Echoes of a lost rhyme.

Once bright, now dimmed to gray,
Fading with each passing day.
Burdened by what I've missed,
In the shadows, they twist.

Faded visions of light,
Drifting beyond my sight.
Heavy lies the remorse,
Flowing with a dark force.

Yet still a flicker glows,
A promise that softly grows.
In the depths of my heart,
I mend each broken part.

From ashes, I will rise,
Reclaiming lost blue skies.
With every tear that streams,
I breathe life to dreams.

Navigating the Inner Cosmos

Stars scatter in my mind,
A universe unconfined.
Galaxies twist and spin,
Where my thoughts begin.

Planets of hopes collide,
In vast oceans of pride.
Nebulas of deep thought,
In silence, they are caught.

Through dark matter I sail,
With courage I prevail.
Comets of joy burst bright,
In the stillness of night.

Waves of sorrow and grace,
Create this endless space.
Eclipses of doubt fade,
In this cosmic parade.

In this journey so grand,
I learn to understand.
Navigating my fears,
Among the stars, my tears.

The Veils of My Being

Layers woven with care,
Each veil a silent prayer.
Hidden depths intertwined,
A tapestry refined.

Fragile threads of my past,
Whisper stories amassed.
Each veil a different hue,
Shading secrets from view.

Beneath the surface lies,
Dreams that reach for the skies.
With every veil I shed,
Old fears are left for dead.

In the light, I stand bold,
Embracing warmth from cold.
With each delicate fold,
New stories to be told.

The veils start to unfurl,
In this beautiful whirl.
Unveiling all I am,
A soul, a heart, a plan.

A Heart's Sanctuary

In silence deep, my spirit breathes,
A refuge found in whispered leaves.
Gentle echoes of the night,
Wrap my heart in soft twilight.

Beneath the stars, my worries cease,
In every shadow, I find peace.
A haven born from love's embrace,
In this sanctuary, I find grace.

Each heartbeat sings a tender song,
Where broken souls can feel they belong.
In the stillness, hope ignites,
As dreams take flight on tranquil nights.

The world outside can drift away,
Here in my heart, forever stay.
A cherished place, my spirit's dome,
Within its walls, I find my home.

Through trials faced and journeys long,
In this embrace, I find my song.
A heart's sanctuary, warm and bright,
Guides me gently into the light.

Finding Home Within

Amidst the chaos, I seek the calm,
A gentle whisper like a soothing balm.
In quiet moments, I come alive,
Finding solace where my heart can thrive.

Within the depths of my wandering soul,
I carve a space that makes me whole.
Memories linger, soft and sweet,
In the chambers where my dreams meet.

Home is not a place, but a feeling,
A warmth that wraps me, ever healing.
In laughter shared and secrets spun,
I find my peace, I'm never done.

Through the storms that shape my way,
I carry love with me each day.
In the embrace of what has been,
I weave my tapestry, finding within.

So here's to journeys, both far and near,
To every heartbeat that draws me near.
In the mirror of my own heart's hue,
I discover the home that's always true.

In the Arms of Solitude

In the arms of solitude, I find my peace,
Where time and chaos momentarily cease.
The world can wait, I breathe and sigh,
In quiet corners, I learn to fly.

Here, shadows dance in soft embrace,
I trace the lines of my own space.
Thoughts untangle like a flowing stream,
In silence, I dare to chase a dream.

Whispers of the night, a tender song,
In solitude's grip, I feel I belong.
With every heartbeat, I grow anew,
Finding strength in the stillness, it's true.

Each moment, a canvas waiting to bloom,
In the solitude, there's room for gloom.
But joy emerges, a brilliant light,
Guiding me through the velvet night.

So I cherish these hours, these tender reprieves,
For in solitude's arms, my spirit believes.
Here, I gather my thoughts, my heart, my will,
In the quiet embrace, I am still.

The Palette of My Soul

Colors splash across a vibrant sky,
Each hue a whisper, a soft goodbye.
A stroke of joy, a dash of pain,
Together they dance in the pouring rain.

With every shade, a story to tell,
From bright sunrises to twilight's bell.
On the canvas of thoughts, I paint my dreams,
In kaleidoscope visions, my spirit gleams.

The reds of passion, the blues of trust,
In every blend, I create what I must.
Greens of growth reach towards the sun,
In this masterpiece, I am one.

Each brush of love, a gentle caress,
In the palette of my heart, I find my nest.
Through every layer, both thick and thin,
My soul reveals what lies within.

So let the colors swirl and collide,
In this vibrant world, I shall abide.
With every heartbeat, I shall compose,
A beautiful life in the art that flows.

The Timeless Within

In the silence of my soul,
Echoes of wisdom flow,
Time drifts like a feather,
In the heart's gentle glow.

Memories dance like shadows,
Whispering tales of yore,
Lessons wrapped in stillness,
Unlocking every door.

Moments that never faded,
Crystals caught in my gaze,
Each heartbeat a reminder,
In life's intricate maze.

The fire within me burns,
Timeless as the sky,
Drawing strength from the ages,
As seasons softly fly.

Beacons of My Voyage

Stars light the vast expanse,
Guiding me through the night,
Waves crash against my dreams,
In the depths, I find light.

Each port holds a story,
Of laughter and of tears,
I gather them like feathers,
In the winds of my years.

The sails catch the promise,
Of horizons yet to see,
With courage in my heart,
I chart my destiny.

Old maps become new paths,
As I journey along,
Beacons of hope surround me,
In the ocean's sweet song.

Anchored in the present,
I embrace the unknown,
With every wave I conquer,
I flourish, I have grown.

The Canvas of My Life

Brush strokes of experience,
Color my every day,
Each hue tells a story,
In the light of my play.

Shadows blend with brilliance,
Creating depth and form,
In the palette of my heart,
My spirit stays warm.

With every drop of pigment,
I craft the dreams I dream,
Layered in vivid honor,
Sculpting my own theme.

The canvas shifts and changes,
As I grow from within,
I paint my path with passion,
Every loss, every win.

Framed by love and laughter,
Each image holds a truth,
I cherish every moment,
In the gallery of youth.

Letting Go of Shadows

Fading whispers in the dusk,
I learn to release the chains,
Embracing all my sorrows,
As the light gently reigns.

Each shadow speaks of burdens,
Of fears I must outgrow,
I gather strength from darkness,
To let my spirit flow.

In the quiet of the night,
I find a place to breathe,
With every star that twinkles,
I weave my heart's reprieve.

The past becomes a canvas,
With colors worn and faded,
As I step into the sun,
All my pain is traded.

Letting go transforms me,
Into the light I soar,
Shadows fade like whispers,
As I embrace what's in store.

The Light Within Shadows

In the quiet of the night,
Stars whisper secrets bright.
Shadows dance, they intertwine,
Yet within them, hope will shine.

The moon casts a gentle glow,
Illuminating paths below.
Every corner, dark and deep,
Holds a promise, dreams to keep.

Against the canvas of the dark,
A flicker sparks, ignites a mark.
From the depths, a voice will rise,
To challenge fears, to touch the skies.

Through the mist, through the haze,
Emerges strength in subtle ways.
For even when the night is long,
The light within will keep us strong.

So embrace the shadows near,
For within them, light is clear.
In each struggle, each great test,
The light within will manifest.

Echoes of My Truth

In the silence, hear the call,
Echoes soft and standing tall.
Truth whispers in the gentle breeze,
Carrying hopes with perfect ease.

Through valleys deep and mountains wide,
Honesty becomes my guide.
With every step, I forge my way,
Painting life in hues of gray.

Reflections dance upon the stream,
Like a fleeting, vivid dream.
Each echo sings of battles fought,
Lessons learned and wisdom sought.

In the chambers of my heart,
Every truth plays its part.
Resounding like a ringing bell,
Echoes weave a timeless spell.

I stand tall, with head held high,
Embracing truths that never die.
For in the echoes, I will find,
The strength to leave the past behind.

The Fortress of Soul

Within the fortress, walls of stone,
A sacred place, I call my own.
Fortified by dreams and grace,
Safety found in this embrace.

Battles waged, and storms that blew,
Yet here I stand, bold and true.
Guarding secrets deep within,
A sanctuary where I win.

Each brick laid with love and care,
Echoes of a heart laid bare.
In this realm, I build my throne,
Rising high, never alone.

With every heartbeat, every breath,
I conquer doubt, defy the death.
The fortress stands against the night,
A beacon strong, a guiding light.

Within these walls, my spirit soars,
Unlocking dreams, opening doors.
For in this space, I find my role,
The everlasting fortress of soul.

Clinging to the Inner Flame

In the shadows, embers glow,
Flickering bright, a heart's soft show.
Clinging tight, I tend the fire,
Fueling dreams, igniting desire.

Each spark holds a story untold,
Whispers of warmth, both brave and bold.
Though winds may howl and doubts arise,
I shield this flame beneath the skies.

Through the trials, through the strife,
The inner flame becomes my life.
A beacon when the night is dark,
Guiding me with that tiny spark.

With every breath, I feel it burn,
A constant light for which I yearn.
Clinging close, through highs and lows,
This inner flame forever glows.

In moments frail, when hope seems slim,
I gather strength from within, not whim.
For clinging to this sacred spark,
Leads me forth, igniting the dark.

The Mirror's Embrace

In silence, I behold my face,
Reflections dance in a sacred space.
Each wrinkle tells a tale of old,
Memories wrapped in silver and gold.

With every glance, I touch my heart,
The journey carved, a work of art.
Whispers echo in the quiet dark,
Lighting shadows, igniting a spark.

Fragments of laughter, traces of tears,
A map unraveled through the years.
The mirror holds my truth so clear,
An echo of all that I hold dear.

In this embrace, I find my peace,
A solemn bond that will never cease.
Reflection of strength and tender grace,
In the mirror's arms, I find my place.

Sanctuary of Self

In the stillness, I retreat to me,
A sanctuary where my spirit's free.
Walls of comfort, painted in light,
Here, my soul takes flight each night.

Thoughts like raindrops on window panes,
Soothing rhythms, releasing pains.
In whispered prayers, I find my ground,
The heart's quiet song, a joyful sound.

With every breath, the world unfurls,
A refuge made of dreams and pearls.
Within these walls, the chaos fades,
Unraveled calm in the deepest shades.

I linger long in this sacred space,
A gentle smile upon my face.
Here I bloom, a flower bold,
In the sanctuary of self, I unfold.

In the Garden of I

Among the blooms, I stroll alone,
In a garden where thoughts are sown.
Petals whisper secrets of the dawn,
Each bud a promise, each stem a song.

With careful hands, I tend my dreams,
Watering hopes with gentle streams.
In shadows deep and sunlight bright,
I gather strength, I seek the light.

The fragrance lingers, sweet and bold,
A tapestry of stories told.
With every season that comes to pass,
New blooms arise from blades of grass.

In this haven, I find my way,
Nurturing joy at the break of day.
In the garden of I, I learn to grow,
Each flower nurtured, each petal aglow.

The Voice Beneath the Noise

In the clamor, I search for peace,
A subtle song that will not cease.
Beyond the chaos, a whisper calls,
Guiding me gently through life's stalls.

Amidst the shouts and bustling crowd,
A sacred truth waits, soft yet loud.
In quiet corners, I close my eyes,
Finding solace where stillness lies.

Each heartbeat sings a soothing tune,
A melody birthed beneath the moon.
With every pulse, the world aligns,
And silence reveals the heart's designs.

In the depths where shadows creep,
The voice beneath the noise, I keep.
A gentle anchor in the storm,
In chaos' grip, I find my form.

Threads of the Heart

In silence weave the dreams we dare,
With gentle whispers, love laid bare.
Each moment stitches time to thread,
A tapestry where souls are fed.

Through colors bright and shadowed hue,
Emotions dance, both old and new.
The fabric holds our joys and fears,
Together sewn, through all the years.

A golden strand, a silver line,
In every twist, our fates entwine.
The heart provides a guiding thread,
In warmth and trust, we are well led.

Fingers trace the patterns spun,
In every heart, we are as one.
Connections strong, though miles apart,
We wear these threads, the threads of heart.

Time may fray some edges keen,
Yet love endures, forever seen.
In every stitch, a story lives,
The threads of heart, the gift it gives.

The Anchor of Solitude

In quiet depths where shadows fall,
I find my peace, I hear the call.
The mind retreats to stillness found,
An anchor firm on solid ground.

With whispered thoughts that softly flow,
I meet the self, and seeds we sow.
In solitude, I plant my dreams,
A world within, or so it seems.

The waves may crash; the storms may roar,
But here I stand, I seek no more.
The heart's own rhythm guides the day,
An anchor holds, come what may.

Through silence deep, I learn to see,
The beauty found in being free.
Each breath a gift, each moment clear,
In solitude, I draw you near.

Embracing stillness, I find light,
In shadows deep, I learn to write.
The anchor of my soul is strong,
In solitude, I find my song.

Shadows of My Past

In corners dark, where echoes dwell,
The shadows whisper tales to tell.
They dance like ghosts in fading light,
Reminding me of wrong and right.

Each memory, a fleeting thought,
In tangled webs, the lessons taught.
Though scars may linger, fade and blend,
The past remains, our faithful friend.

Through winding paths, I used to tread,
With footsteps soft, while hope was led.
The shadows cast, a haunting grace,
Yet in their depths, I find my place.

A reflection that forever stays,
The shadows guide in quiet ways.
They shape my heart, they mold my soul,
In every loss, I find the whole.

Embrace the past, for it has taught,
A journey great, though battles fought.
In shadows dark, my strength amassed,
I stand renewed, despite the past.

Embrace of the Self

In quiet moments, still and deep,
I find the self, the truth I keep.
No masks to wear, just me alone,
In love's embrace, I find my home.

The mirror gleams, a sacred space,
Reflecting all, my truest grace.
With open arms, I greet my flaws,
In every crack, my spirit draws.

Through trials faced, the pain and strife,
I learn to honor this sweet life.
Embracing all, the light and shade,
In every breath, new dreams are made.

The whisper soft, the heart's own plea,
To love the self, to simply be.
In every heartbeat, I am whole,
The embrace of self, my worth, my goal.

So dance with me, through joy and tears,
In every moment, shed your fears.
With arms wide open, let love swell,
In the embrace of self, all is well.

The Cloak of Authenticity

In shadows deep, I find the light,
A cloak of truth, now feels so right.
It wraps around my weary soul,
Unveiling dreams that make me whole.

With every sigh, I shed the guise,
Embracing flaws, I rise and rise.
The mirror reflects a heart anew,
In every fault, there's strength I grew.

The world may push, it may contest,
But in this skin, I feel the best.
I walk among the crowd of masks,
Released from doubt, the quiet asks.

As I unravel layer by layer,
The whispers fade, the doubt becomes air.
With courage stoked, I take my stand,
Authentically, I claim this land.

In fabric soft, my truth is sewn,
With threads of hope, I'm not alone.
Each step I take, this journey vast,
In my true self, I find my past.

My Inner Sanctuary

In silence deep, I find my peace,
A sanctuary where doubts cease.
With every breath, I nurture calm,
A gentle brook, my soothing balm.

The world outside can roar and spin,
But in this space, I feel within.
Walls of flesh cannot contain
The vast expanse of love and pain.

Each thought I weave, a sacred thread,
In quiet moments, fears are shed.
With open heart, I welcome light,
In my sanctuary, all feels right.

Where memories dance, and dreams take flight,
I gather strength, dispelling night.
With every whisper, I reclaim
The essence lost, igniting flame.

This inner realm, a treasure rare,
I'll guard with love, with utmost care.
In solitude, I find the muse,
In my own heart, I shall not lose.

The Confines of Comfort

Within the bounds, I find my ease,
A gentle grip, a subtle tease.
Yet comfort's chains can hold me tight,
Restraining growth, dimming the light.

Each cozy nook, a lullaby,
Temptation whispers, 'Stay nearby.'
But in the dark, a voice will call,
To journey forth, to rise, to fall.

The fear of change, it claws and bites,
Yet still I dream of distant heights.
Though safe and sound, my heart will ache,
To step outside, I must awake.

With trembling hands, I dare to strive,
To break these chains, to feel alive.
For comfort's arms may feel divine,
But growth awaits beyond the line.

So here I stand, on edges bold,
With stories waiting to be told.
In courage found, new worlds unfold,
Beyond the comforts, I'll be gold.

Weaving My Narrative

With threads of joy and strands of pain,
I weave my story through sun and rain.
Each stitch a mark of lessons learned,
In vibrant hues, my passions burned.

The fabric rich, with tales to share,
Adventures bold, and moments rare.
In every fold, a twist of fate,
Crafting dreams that won't abate.

With heart in hand, I spin my tale,
Through mountains high and valleys pale.
In every choice, a choice to grow,
With every fray, my truths will flow.

A tapestry of hopes and fears,
Embracing laughter, shedding tears.
In every loop, I find my grace,
My narrative, my sacred space.

So onward I weave, through thick and thin,
In colors bright, my journey's win.
A legacy of love entwined,
In woven tales, my heart defined.

Scripting My Own Destiny

With each word, I carve my fate,
A canvas pure, I'll decorate.
Stars align in daring dreams,
Guiding me to brighter themes.

No chains can bind this soaring heart,
Each step I take, a brand new start.
Through storms and trials, I will stand,
In truth's embrace, I'll make my plan.

The whispers of my soul are clear,
Within my heart, I hold no fear.
Paths unknown, I boldly tread,
With faith as fuel, I'll forge ahead.

A book unwritten, page turned bright,
Each moment holds a spark of light.
With courage sewn into my seams,
I'll turn my hopes into real dreams.

And when the twilight starts to fall,
I rise, I shine, I hear the call.
The story's mine, with ink of gold,
A legacy of dreams foretold.

In the Echo of Silence

In quiet moments, truth does speak,
A gentle breeze, a tender leak.
Whispers soft, like petals fall,
In silence pure, I hear it call.

The world outside may rush and roar,
Yet in my heart, I seek for more.
In shadows deep, there's peace to find,
A sacred space for heart and mind.

Each note of calm, a melody,
That dances lightly, setting free.
In stillness, echoes gently blend,
A timeless song that has no end.

Through silence, I become aware,
Of dreams that linger in the air.
In echoes, life's soft stories play,
In the still night, I find my way.

So let the world spin fast and loud,
I linger here, unfazed and proud.
In the echo of silence, I'll create,
A symphony that feels like fate.

The Flame of Self-Affirmation

In every breath, I claim my worth,
A fire ignites, a vibrant birth.
With every step, I stake my claim,
In shadows cast, I fan the flame.

No doubt shall dim this radiant light,
I rise, I glow, embracing the fight.
With words of strength, I build my tower,
Empowered by my inner power.

Each heartache's just a stepping stone,
My spirit's fierce, forever grown.
In moments when the world feels cold,
I stoke the flame of strength untold.

I nourish dreams with tender care,
With every spark, my courage flares.
In self-belief, the magic blooms,
Dispelling all the heavy glooms.

So here I stand, a blazing star,
In my own light, I've come so far.
The flame of me will shine so bright,
An anthem born of pure delight.

Whispers of My Essence

Deep within, a voice does rise,
A symphony of whispered ties.
The essence flows, a river wide,
In every heartbeat, there's a guide.

Through tangled paths, I seek to know,
The roots of all that I let grow.
Each gentle sigh, a truth unveiled,
In quiet moments, I've prevailed.

The essence speaks in colors bright,
It paints my world with pure delight.
With every whisper, I connect,
To wisdom's light, I stand erect.

In subtle tones, my spirit sings,
A melody of hidden things.
Through layers deep, I unearth grace,
In the whispers, I find my place.

So here I stand, embraced by me,
With open heart, I choose to be.
The whispers of my essence flow,
A dance of light, forever glow.

Cherishing the Forgotten Echoes

In shadows deep, whispers reside,
Memories linger, time's gentle guide.
Pathways untold, where silence speaks,
Fragments of laughter, the heart still seeks.

Ancient corners, the stories thrive,
Faded photographs made alive.
In every corner, echoes play,
Reminding me of yesterday.

The golden light, a fleeting guest,
In every heartbeat, a quiet quest.
To cherish the tales, the lost, the found,
In silence, the echoes are profound.

Amongst the ruins where time stands still,
I find comfort, a silent thrill.
Through every sorrow, through every joy,
The echoes linger, never to destroy.

In the tapestry of what once was clear,
The forgotten whispers hold me near.
As I embrace what time forgot,
These cherished echoes connect the dot.

The Sanctuary of Self

In the stillness, I find my voice,
In shadows of doubt, I make my choice.
A sanctuary found within deep space,
In quiet moments, I seek my grace.

Walls of the heart, strong yet kind,
Within their bounds, peace I find.
A fragile world, yet ever so bold,
In this refuge, my spirit unfolds.

The gentle rains, they wash away,
The burdens that haunt, the fears that sway.
In solitude's arms, I dance with light,
Finding my way, through darkest night.

Each breath a promise, a soothing balm,
In chaos outside, I nurture calm.
The whispers of dreams, they call my name,
In this sanctuary, I stoke the flame.

Through the journey, I claim my truth,
In the heart's embrace, I regain my youth.
A sanctuary forged with every tear,
In every heartbeat, I hold it dear.

Keeping the Flame Alive

In the still of night, embers glow,
A flickering light, a steady flow.
With every breath, I fan the blaze,
In the quiet hours, my spirit stays.

Through storms that rage, through winds that bite,
I carry the flame, my guiding light.
Against the shadows, I stand and fight,
For in my heart, there burns a right.

The whispers of hope, they dance and twirl,
In the darkest corners, they softly swirl.
With every step, I stoke the fire,
In every challenge, I rise higher.

Tales of resilience, etched in time,
Every struggle becomes a rhyme.
Keeping the flame through endless night,
For in its glow, the world feels bright.

As sunsets meld into evening's hue,
I gather strength, I start anew.
Each flicker a promise, a story told,
In keeping the flame, I find my gold.

Reclaiming My Harmony

In the chaos, I seek the sound,
A melody lost, where hope is found.
Each shattered note, a piece of me,
In reclaiming joy, I set it free.

The rhythm of life, a dance so sweet,
In every beat, my heart will greet.
Through trials faced, I find the tune,
Reclaiming my song, under the moon.

Within the quiet, whispers arise,
The symphony waits beneath the skies.
With open arms, I welcome fate,
In reclaiming harmony, I elevate.

From broken strings, new music blooms,
A serenade that dispels the glooms.
In every sigh, a note of grace,
In reclaiming my balance, I find my place.

The harmony flows, unbroken, clear,
In every moment, I hold it dear.
Embracing the journey, the twists and bends,
In reclaiming my harmony, the song never ends.

Fragments of Self

Shattered pieces lie about,
In corners of my mind.
Each fragment tells a story,
Of what I've left behind.

A whisper of the past,
In colors bold and bright.
I gather them together,
To craft my own sunrise.

The canvas of my heart,
Painted with fears and dreams.
Layer by layer I build,
A truth that softly gleams.

In every crack and crevice,
Lies a spark of my soul.
With every stitch I weave,
I feel myself become whole.

So here I stand, unbroken,
Embracing all I am.
Each fragment is a treasure,
In this vast, delicate plan.

In the Mirror's Embrace

Gazing deep into the glass,
Reflections twist and turn.
I see both light and shadow,
As I silently discern.

The eyes that gaze back at me,
Hold secrets yet untold.
In moments of still silence,
A story starts to unfold.

Every wrinkle carries wisdom,
Each smile, a tale of time.
I embrace the lines of laughter,
As I journey and climb.

In the mirror's calm embrace,
I find both grief and grace.
With open heart, I welcome,
All echoes I can face.

This dance of light and shadow,
Creates a picture true.
In this sacred moment,
I discover the real me.

Capturing My Soul's Light

With brush against the canvas,
I paint my hidden glow.
Every stroke a whisper,
Of how my spirit flows.

Colors mingle freely,
Like laughter in the air.
I capture fleeting moments,
In the realm of simple care.

The sunlight forms a silhouette,
Of dreams that dance and play.
I hold them in my heartbeat,
As twilight greets the day.

Through strokes both bold and tender,
I weave my heart's delight.
Each color tells a story,
Of my soul's eternal flight.

And when the world feels heavy,
I'll turn to art and song.
In creation, I find freedom,
Where all my joys belong.

Anchored in the Storm

Waves crash against my spirit,
As tempests swirl around.
Yet in this wild chaos,
I stand firm on solid ground.

Raindrops fall like whispers,
Each one a subtle plea.
The wind may howl and thunder,
But still, I dare to be.

Roots deep in the earth's embrace,
I feel my courage rise.
With every surge of ocean,
I lift my gaze to skies.

The storm may test my patience,
But I will not let go.
In the eye of this whirlwind,
I find my inner glow.

So bring on fierce tempests,
And lightning's fierce display.
For anchored in my essence,
I will not drift away.

Captive to Dreams

In the silence of the night, I soar,
Chasing visions, forevermore.
Soft whispers call me by name,
A flicker of hope, igniting the flame.

Stars illuminate the shadows beneath,
Threads of desire weave dreams with teeth.
In realms where time drifts away,
I find my heart, there I will stay.

Every heartbeat, a silent song,
In worlds of wonder, I belong.
With each dawn, they fade from view,
Yet in my soul, they feel so true.

Resilient, I yearn for the light,
Guided by wishes, taking flight.
A tale of magic, a hope that streams,
Forever captured, I am in dreams.

Beyond the space where shadows flee,
In the echo of all that could be.
I hold my dreams like fragile seams,
Unraveled gently, woven in dreams.

Emblems of Endurance

Rising up from ashes grey,
A testament to another day.
Through storms that whip and winds that howl,
We stand our ground, we never scowl.

Mountains tremble beneath our stride,
Yet in our hearts, we host our pride.
With every bruise, a story told,
Each tear a gem, a heart of gold.

In the face of doubt, we find our spark,
Lighting the way through the dark.
As echoes of our battles fade,
We find the strength we somehow made.

With roots like iron, we dig in deep,
Nurtured with hope, never to weep.
Emblems of grit, scarred and bold,
In the tapestry of life, we unfold.

Through shifting sands and tempest's roar,
We claim our story forevermore.
Resilient hearts that rise and stand,
Together we forge, hand in hand.

The Art of Staying True

In a world of whispers and deceit,
I walk my path, steady on my feet.
With every step, I choose my way,
The art of self, in light of day.

Voices clamor, trying to sway,
Yet in my core, I find my stay.
Honesty blooms like wildflowers bright,
Guiding my soul through the night.

Integrity's song sings loud and clear,
Echoes of truth, I hold near.
With every test, I stand my ground,
In the quiet, my strength is found.

With every choice, a shadow cast,
I rise anew, my spirit amassed.
For in the art of staying true,
I craft the life I'm meant to pursue.

Through passages dark, I will endure,
With courage and love, my heart is sure.
In the mirror of life, I see my view,
A masterpiece forged, in colors anew.

My Voice in the Wilderness

Amid the trees, I raise my call,
Echoing deep, I will not fall.
With every whisper, the wild replies,
In harmony beneath open skies.

The wind carries tales of old,
In every gust, a truth unfolds.
From mountaintop to valley low,
My voice resounds, it will not slow.

In solitude, a strength I find,
Nature's embrace, gentle and kind.
Each note I sing, a beacon bright,
Guiding those lost toward the light.

Through the brambles, I weave my way,
With roots of courage, I'll never sway.
For in this wilderness, I've found my place,
In every shadow, a warm embrace.

My voice in the wild, a sacred sound,
Resonates deeply, unbound, profound.
Through every echo, I stake my claim,
In the wilderness, I'll carve my name.

The Tapestry of Being

In threads of light we weave our days,
Each moment a stitch, in myriad ways.
Colors blend and shadows blend,
A tapestry formed, love to extend.

Whispers of dreams in every fold,
Stories of the young and the old.
The patterns shift with each new breath,
In this fabric, life conquers death.

Textures telling of joy and pain,
The quiet moments, the pouring rain.
Woven tightly, yet free to roam,
In this creation, we find our home.

Unity found in this intricate lace,
Each fragment a part, a sacred space.
Bound by the threads that time has spun,
In the tapestry of being, we are one.

Roots of Resilience

Deep in the earth, a strength we find,
Hidden from sight, yet so well-defined.
Beneath the surface, they stretch and grow,
Roots of resilience, steady and low.

Through storms and droughts, they bend and sway,
Holding the ground, come what may.
In silence, they speak of strength and grace,
A testament found in each growing place.

The leaves above dance with the breeze,
Yet the roots below work hard to please.
Drawing from depths where the darkness sleeps,
In resilience, the heart of the forest keeps.

Nurtured by trials, shaped by strife,
These roots of ours hold stories of life.
In every challenge, they firmly stand,
A reminder that strength is often unplanned.

Fragments of Identity

Scattered pieces, a jigsawed whole,
A dance of colors that fill the soul.
Each shard reflecting a different hue,
In the fragments, the self starts anew.

Memories etched in gentle lines,
Whispers of dreams under starlit signs.
The laughter, the tears, all interlace,
Carving the paths that we dare to face.

Voices entwined in a chorus of time,
Each note plays a part, a unique rhyme.
From histories rich to futures bright,
In fragments of identity, we find our light.

A mosaic growing with every chance,
Finding our rhythm, we learn to dance.
Celebrating chaos, we rise and fall,
In every fragment, the truth stands tall.

Embrace of the Unseen

In shadows cast by the light so bright,
The unseen holds secrets, hidden from sight.
A soft embrace, tender and warm,
In the silence, we find a calm charm.

Whispers of love in the air around,
In the gentlest touch, connections abound.
Beyond the vision, the heart can see,
In the embrace of the unseen, we are free.

The quiet moments, the breaths we share,
Carried by currents, an unspoken prayer.
In every heartbeat, a rhythm divine,
The unseen pulls us, a cosmic design.

Let go of doubt, embrace the unknown,
In the depths, seeds of trust have grown.
In this dance of shadows, light shall glean,
We find our truth in the unseen.

Threads of Resilience

In shadows deep, we weave our dreams,
Through trials faced, or so it seems.
Each thread a story, rich and bright,
With colors born from endless fight.

Through storms we stand, through tears we grow,
Hold tight the flame, let courage glow.
With every stitch, a tale unfolds,
In tapestry, our strength beholds.

The past may haunt, but hope is near,
We find our voice, we choose to cheer.
Together, strong, we face the night,
For in our hearts, we hold the light.

Each scar a mark, each wound a guide,
In unity, we will abide.
Unraveling fears, we rise anew,
Threads of resilience, binding true.

Embracing the Echoes

In the silence, whispers blend,
Echoes of love that never end.
Each memory holds a gentle grace,
In shadows, we find a warm embrace.

Time flows softly, a river wide,
Carving paths where dreams reside.
Voices linger, calling clear,
In their cadence, we draw near.

Every moment, a melody sweet,
With every heartbeat, we feel complete.
Dancing through the rhythm of night,
Embracing echoes, we take flight.

Bound by the stories, old and new,
In each echo, a part of you.
Together we sing, forever strong,
In the refrain, we all belong.

The Weight of My Essence

Beneath the surface, soft yet bold,
The weight of my essence, glimmers gold.
Each heartbeat echoes, a symphony,
A story woven, uniquely me.

With every breath, I embrace the fight,
Through shadows cast, I seek the light.
In stillness found, my spirit flies,
Breaking boundaries, touching skies.

The journey long, but worth the cost,
For in my heart, nothing is lost.
Each tear a river, each laugh a star,
The weight of my essence, who we are.

Together we carry the dreams we share,
The weight of my essence, light as air.
In unity, we rise and shine,
A tapestry of souls entwined.

Clinging to Whispers

In the quiet, whispers roam,
Carrying secrets, leading home.
Each sigh a story, soft and clear,
Clinging to whispers, we persevere.

In the dusk, the world slows down,
Amidst the noise, we wear our crown.
A gentle breeze, a soothing sound,
In whispers, strength is often found.

Voices dance like leaves in flight,
Guiding us through the darkest night.
In their tone, we find our way,
Clinging to whispers of a new day.

With every word, hope is born,
In shared moments, never worn.
Together we rise, hearts aligned,
Clinging to whispers, forever entwined.

Embers of My Essence

In the quiet glow of night,
Flickers dance, a soft delight.
Whispers of a burning past,
Echoes of shadows, unsurpassed.

Fleeting moments, soft yet bright,
Memories ignited, take their flight.
Each spark a story yet untold,
In warmth of hearth, dreams unfold.

Winds of change may shift the flame,
But embers stay, though not the same.
An inner warmth, a glowing heart,
In every pulse, the flame a part.

Through the darkness, I will rise,
With burning passion, shape the skies.
A journey forged in fiery hues,
A testament to all I choose.

In this dance of light and shade,
I embrace the paths I've made.
Each ember glows with essence true,
In every breath, I find my due.

Threads of Self

Tangled fibers, woven tight,
Colorful strands that catch the light.
Each thread tells a tale unique,
In the tapestry, I seek.

Fragile whispers in the weave,
A history that I believe.
Twisted knots, a story told,
In every hue, my heart of gold.

Pulling gently, letting go,
Understanding what I know.
Each connection, strong yet slight,
Bringing pieces into sight.

In this fabric, I reside,
The vibrant shades I cannot hide.
Interwoven dreams and fears,
Together stitched through all the years.

Threads of laughter, threads of tears,
In their embrace, I face my fears.
Each moment a vital part,
In this quilt, I find my heart.

Anchored in Reflection

Still waters calm, a mirror gleams,
In its depths, I find my dreams.
Anchored here, a safe retreat,
In quietude, my heart's heartbeat.

Ripples whisper tales of yore,
Memories surfacing ashore.
In the silence, wisdom grows,
With every thought, a river flows.

Fragments of a fractured past,
In this haven, peace is cast.
Each ripple carries lessons learned,
In the stillness, I discerned.

The weight of time, a gentle guide,
In reflection, I confide.
Through ebbing tides and rising moons,
I find my voice in quiet tunes.

Anchored deep, I stand my ground,
In the stillness, strength is found.
With every glance, I see more clear,
In this moment, I persevere.

Whispers of My Core

Softly spoken in the night,
Echos dance with soft delight.
Deep within, a voice so pure,
In its warmth, I find my cure.

Rhythms pulse beneath my skin,
In stillness, the truth begins.
Whispers brush against my soul,
In their embrace, I feel whole.

Fragments of the heart, they sing,
Carrying hope in gentle wing.
Unraveling secrets, layer by layer,
In every whisper, love's true player.

A gentle breeze through sacred space,
In the silence, I find grace.
In the whispers, I am known,
In their warmth, my seeds are sown.

Every murmur, rich and deep,
In their softness, dreams do leap.
Whispers of my core remain,
In their echo, I find my gain.

Coalescing with the Stars

In the quiet night, we gaze so high,
Whispers of light, dancing in the sky.
Each twinkle a tale, every blink a dream,
We reach for the heavens, lost in their gleam.

The cosmos hums softly, an ancient song,
Binding our souls where we always belong.
Galaxies swirl with a celestial grace,
In their vast embrace, we find our place.

Fingers of stardust trace paths of time,
Constellations shining, their stories rhyme.
We blend with the night, becoming the light,
Infinite wonders in the heart of the night.

As the darkness deepens, we soar ever free,
Connected with all in this universe spree.
With each heartbeat sync, we learn how to fly,
Together we rise, like sparks in the sky.

And when dawn breaks softly, a new day unfurls,
The stars turn to whispers, as we embrace worlds.
In the light of the sun, we'll carry the glow,
For we are the stardust, and we'll never let go.

The Lighthouse Within

In the heart's harbor, a beacon stands tall,
Guiding lost sailors, heeding their call.
Its light pierces fog, dispelling the night,
Showcasing the path through the stormy fright.

Waves crash against rocks, relentless and wild,
Yet the lighthouse stands firm, ever unbeguiled.
Its warmth so inviting, a signal of home,
In tempestuous seas, we are never alone.

Shadows may linger, but hope always glows,
A flicker of faith where the dark wind blows.
Through trials and struggles, my spirit is free,
For the lighthouse within, always shines for me.

Each night brings a lesson, each dawn brings a chance,
To dance with the currents, to dream and to prance.
With courage, I wander wherever I roam,
Knowing within me, I've built my own home.

And though storms may rage, and the skies turn to gray,
The lighthouse within me will light up the way.
So here I will stand, steadfast and bright,
A beacon of hope in the long, endless night.

Starlit Paths of Memory

As twilight descends, a blanket of night,
I wander through paths where the stars are bright.
Each step brings a whisper, a tale to unfold,
Remnants of moments, both cherished and bold.

Past laughter and tears, I travel with grace,
In the glow of the moon, I find my own space.
Every flicker of light, a memory's glow,
A tapestry woven, where feelings still flow.

With shadows as friends, the night carries words,
Notes of forgotten songs, soft as the birds.
Collecting the echoes of years gone by,
Starlit paths guide me through the silent sky.

In the heart of the night, I reclaim what was lost,
Each step a reminder of love and its cost.
Embracing the silence, the stillness I find,
Among starlit paths, my soul is aligned.

And when dawn appears, washing dreams into day,
I carry the starlight, it never will stray.
In the depths of my being, the memories shine,
Forever reminding me, I'm eternally twined.

Portrait of My Inner Landscape

A canvas of feelings, painted in hue,
Swirls of emotion, both vibrant and blue.
Each brushstroke a story, each color a sigh,
Reflecting the depths of my heart's private sky.

Mountains of hope rise, touching the sun,
While valleys of doubt whisper 'you're done'.
Yet in this vast stretch, I learn to embrace,
The light and the shadow, each given a place.

Streams of creativity flow through my veins,
Carving through pathways, erasing the chains.
In the forest of thoughts, I wander and roam,
Finding the peace that leads me back home.

Flowers of passion bloom wild in my chest,
Each petal a dream I believe is the best.
While roots intertwine, anchoring me deep,
In the soil of my essence, where treasures I keep.

The horizon unfolds, a blend of the light,
As I paint my existence, unyielding and bright.
For in this portrait, my spirit can soar,
Every stroke a reminder of the strength I adore.

Dances with Dissonance

In shadows where silence sways,
Footfalls echo, a muted craze.
A waltz of whispers, restless hearts,
With every step, the tension starts.

Caught in the pull of sweet despair,
Notes clash like thunder in the air.
Twisted melodies, lost in time,
A symphony, broken yet sublime.

The dance begins, a fiery plight,
In twilight's glow, we chase the night.
Swaying softly, we lose and find,
In dissonance, our souls entwined.

Each turn reveals a hidden truth,
In discord lies the spark of youth.
With every leap, we rise and fall,
Embracing chaos, we hear the call.

Through the storm, though voices clash,
We write our tale in every flash.
Dances weave through tears and laughter,
In disarray, we forge after.

Memories in a Raindrop

Each drop that falls, a tale retold,
Echoes of warmth in the damp and cold.
They shimmer bright, on windows gleam,
Carrying whispers of a distant dream.

Puddles gather, reflecting the sky,
Footsteps traced where we used to lie.
Ripples form, where laughter rang,
Time captured in each soft twang.

A moment held, then swept away,
As currents drift and shadows play.
The scent of earth, the taste of rain,
Awakens memories of joy and pain.

Through storms we danced, entwined as one,
Under grey skies, we had our fun.
Each tear that fell in the pouring night,
Became a star in the fading light.

So let it rain, let the memories flow,
For every drop, a chance to grow.
In every storm, a story lies,
In raindrops, love never dies.

My Spirit's Compass

In the quiet, my heart does roam,
Seeking the path that leads me home.
Each beat a guide, a gentle nudge,
Through tangled woods, I will not budge.

A whisper calls from the depths within,
Fueling the fire where journeys begin.
Stars align in the midnight sky,
With every twinkle, I learn to fly.

Mountains rise, and rivers bend,
But restless winds shall be my friend.
Guided by light, with purpose clear,
My spirit's compass will steer me near.

When doubts assail and shadows creep,
In silent moments, my faith runs deep.
Each step I take, though unknown,
On this path, I'm never alone.

Through valleys low and heights so grand,
I trust in the pull of a steady hand.
For every turn, a lesson learned,
My spirit's compass, ever returned.

The Language of Longing

In the silence, a heartbeat sighs,
Words unspoken hide in the skies.
A longing glance, a furtive touch,
In stillness, we speak, we say so much.

Fingers tracing the lines of fate,
Whispers linger, never too late.
In the spaces where wishes bloom,
Desire dances in the gloom.

The eyes convey what lips won't say,
In the twilight, we find our way.
Every glance, a silent plea,
Yearning grips us, wild and free.

Through shadows cast, we navigate,
Chasing dreams that almost elate.
Between breaths, our worlds collide,
In longing's arms, we confide.

The language of longing, soft and bold,
Is stitched in hearts of silver and gold.
For in every pause, a story is spun,
In this sweet silence, we are one.

The Map of My Journey

Winding roads and endless skies,
Stories etched where silence lies.
Footprints trace my steps so bold,
Each turn reveals a tale retold.

Mountains high and valleys deep,
In the heart, my secrets keep.
Guided by the stars so bright,
Every path a dance of light.

Rivers flow and oceans roar,
Every wave leads to the shore.
Cartographer of dreams I find,
Maps of memory intertwined.

Through storms and skies of blue,
Facing fears, embracing true.
In every mile, the fire glows,
The map of life in colors flows.

So here's to journeys fresh and grand,
To laughter shared and outstretched hand.
With every step, my heart does sing,
The map unfolds, with hope it brings.

The Glow of Inner Light

In shadows cast, a whisper glows,
A flicker bright where spirit flows.
Within the depths, a flame ignites,
A beacon shines through darkest nights.

Though storms may rage and fears might rise,
The inner light will never disguise.
With courage drawn from depths unknown,
A quiet strength within me grown.

Through every trial, pain, and strife,
This radiant glow brings me to life.
In moments dim, it guides my way,
A warmth that never fades to gray.

The heart's true compass, gentle spark,
Illumines paths, ignites the dark.
In solitude, I find my grace,
The glow resides in every space.

So let it shine, this gift so rare,
A glow of hope in every prayer.
From within, the light will soar,
A vibrant dance forevermore.

Breath Beneath the Surface

In quiet depths, a pulse resides,
Beneath the tide where secret hides.
Each breath a wave, each sigh a sea,
A rhythm flows, unbound and free.

Beneath the calm, a tempest brews,
In silent spaces, whispers muse.
The surface shines, yet depths call out,
Inviting dreams, inviting doubt.

With every breath, I dive anew,
Finding treasures in the blue.
The currents pull, the waves embrace,
In every plunge, I find my place.

In the depths, where shadows play,
I learn to dance, I learn to sway.
With every heartbeat, the world unfolds,
A tapestry of stories told.

The breath beneath, a sacred space,
Where silence echoes, time's warm grace.
In every ripple, life reframes,
Breath beneath, a dance of names.

The Essence of Persistence

In the face of every wall,
Resilience rises, answering the call.
Each stumble met with iron will,
The essence strong, my heart's fulfilled.

With every setback, seeds are sown,
In barren ground, new faith is grown.
For dreams may fade but never die,
In the struggle, learn to fly.

The storms may come and doubts may creep,
Yet in my soul, a promise deep.
Persistence fuels the fire within,
A truth that lies beneath my skin.

Through trials faced and battles fought,
In every lesson, wisdom's sought.
Unyielding spirit, fierce and bright,
The essence of my inner fight.

So here's to those who dare to stand,
Who grasp the dreams with steady hand.
Through every challenge, hearts shall soar,
The essence of persistence, forevermore.

Embracing My Truth

In the mirror, I see my soul,
Reflections of scars, making me whole.
Each tear a lesson, each smile a light,
In the depths of darkness, I find my might.

I shed the masks, let the colors blaze,
Living unapologetically, through life's maze.
With every heartbeat, I'm shedding the doubt,
In a world of noise, I choose to shout.

Embracing the stories that shaped my core,
With open arms, I welcome what's in store.
The whispers of doubt fade into the past,
Each moment a treasure, too precious to cast.

In the silence, my heart takes flight,
Learning to dance in the soft moonlight.
My truth my compass, my guiding star,
Radiating love, no matter how far.

Boldly I stand, my spirit unveiled,
With courage within, I shall not be derailed.
This is my journey, this is my song,
In embracing my truth, I finally belong.

Tides of Introspection

Waves crash softly against the shore,
Whispers of secrets I yearn to explore.
The ocean reflects my feelings inside,
In the tidal pull, my thoughts collide.

Each ebb and flow, a moment in time,
Navigating emotions, like mountains to climb.
The current drags me, deep and profound,
In the depths of my mind, new treasures are found.

As I dive deeper into the sea's embrace,
In the shadows of silence, I find my place.
The tides will teach me, the breezes will guide,
In the vastness of waters, I no longer hide.

I gather my strength from the colors I see,
Unraveling layers that once burdened me.
The rhythm of nature, a calming release,
In unity, I find my inner peace.

The waves will recede, and the shores will change,
And yet through it all, I'll rearrange.
With each passing tide, I grow and I learn,
In the dance of introspection, my spirit will burn.

Holding the Invisible

In the quiet moments, I sense what's there,
The weight of affection, hanging in the air.
Invisible threads connecting our hearts,
In the tapestry woven, love never parts.

With every heartbeat, I cradle the unseen,
In a world of whispers, what could have been.
The warmth of a touch, though miles apart,
In the realm of the spirit, we share one heart.

Each thought of you is a spark that ignites,
On a canvas of dreams, we soar to new heights.
Holding the invisible, courage to trust,
In the silence, our bond becomes a must.

Through shadows and doubts, I continue to hold,
A love that's resilient, and never grows cold.
In the realm of the unseen lies strength untold,
Together we flourish, in life's grand unfold.

In every heartbeat, a promise I sense,
Building connections that are truly immense.
Holding the invisible, our spirits entwine,
In the sacred space, forever you're mine.

The Pulse of My Spirit

In the rhythm of life, I hear a sound,
The pulse of my spirit beats all around.
With every moment, I'm learning to flow,
In the dance of my heart, I continue to grow.

The vibrant beat echoes in the night,
Guiding my journey, igniting my light.
With passion as fuel, I soar and I dive,
In the pulse of my spirit, I truly survive.

Emotions like waves, they rise and then fall,
Tuning my essence to the cosmos' call.
With each heartbeat, I find my way back,
In the melody whispered, I'll never lack.

Through the trials and triumphs, I'll find my beat,
In the song of my spirit, life feels complete.
A chorus of love plays softly within,
Each note a reminder, I'm destined to win.

The pulse of my spirit, a beacon so bright,
Illuminating paths in the dead of night.
With every heartbeat, I rise and I sing,
In the rhythm of life, my spirit takes wing.

Resilience in the Storm

Amid the raging tempest's howl,
I stand firm with strength and vow.
Waves may crash, yet I remain,
In every loss, there's hope to gain.

With every gust, I feel the fight,
Roots hold deep through darkest night.
The storm may roar, but in my chest,
Resilience blooms, my spirit's quest.

The sky may darken, clouds may swell,
But in my heart, a light doth dwell.
Through trials faced and mountains climbed,
A warrior's heart, forever primed.

I rise anew with every fall,
A whisper soft, yet fierce growth calls.
Nature shows what's deep within,
In chaos, I find strength to begin.

So let the winds rage, let them blow,
For in this storm, my roots will grow.
With every challenge, I will strive,
Resilience breathes, and I'll survive.

In the Eye of My Universe

In stillness found, I gaze within,
A universe where dreams begin.
Stars align in patterns bright,
Bringing dawn to the velvet night.

Thoughts like comets streak through space,
Each dream igniting a silent grace.
In the eye, I find my core,
A boundless realm, forevermore.

Moments swirl like galaxies spin,
In the quiet, my soul's akin.
Luminous paths that guide my way,
In this void, I choose to stay.

Every heartbeat echoes strong,
In this sanctuary, I belong.
Gravity pulls, yet I soar high,
In my universe, I'll never shy.

So I cherish this silent space,
Where hope and love find their place.
In the eye, I'll always be,
The architect of my decree.

From Ashes to Wholeness

From the ashes, I rise anew,
With every fragment, strength I drew.
What was lost, now sparks ignite,
Rebuilding dreams in soft twilight.

Each scar I wear, a story told,
Of battles fought and moments bold.
Turning pain into golden thread,
A tapestry of life ahead.

With every breath, I weave and twine,
Resilient heart, like intertwining vine.
From remnants scattered, hope makes whole,
A phoenix born, reclaiming soul.

The fire that burned now fuels my flame,
In the dance of life, I find my name.
Ashes whisper of what's to be,
A journey forged, eternally free.

So I gather pieces, one by one,
Reviving dreams, a life begun.
From ashes deep, I raise my head,
In wholeness found, no longer fled.

The Pulse of Existence

In every heart, a rhythm plays,
A pulse that dances through our days.
Each beat a whisper, clear and true,
The essence of life flows fresh as dew.

From mountains high to oceans deep,
Nature sings and shadows leap.
In every moment, presence flows,
The pulse that binds, with sweetness glows.

Synapses fire, dreams come alive,
In this sacred dance, we strive.
Connected threads, both near and far,
We are the rhythm, each a star.

With open hands, we feel the waves,
The pulse of love that gently saves.
In laughter shared and tears we weep,
Existence calls us, deep and steep.

So let us dance to life's great song,
In unity where we belong.
The pulse of existence, fierce and free,
In every heart, a symphony.

Anchors in the Tide

Waves crash against the shore,
Whispers of the ocean's lore.
Silent ships in twilight gleam,
Anchored deep in sunset's dream.

Wind carries tales of the sea,
Where sailors yearn to be free.
Stars above begin to shine,
Guiding hearts on paths divine.

Tides rise and fall like breath,
In the dance of life and death.
Hope anchored in every soul,
As we strive to feel whole.

Footprints fading in the sand,
Time's tide erases every brand.
Yet memories linger bright,
Illuminated by moonlight.

Through storms and tranquil nights,
We find strength in our heights.
Anchors hold, though seas may rage,
Love writes our story on the page.

The Resonance of My Heart

In silence, I hear your name,
Echoes soft, yet never tame.
Rhythms dance in twilight's glow,
Pulse of passion, ebb and flow.

Notes entwine like branches fair,
Heartstrings plucked with tender care.
Each beat sings a tale untold,
Melodies that never grow old.

With every breath, a symphony,
Crafted deep in you and me.
As time bends and stretches wide,
Love's music is our shared guide.

Chords of laughter, shades of tears,
Resonate through all our years.
In the silence, hear the art,
The sweet resonance of the heart.

Let the echoes lead us home,
In each moment, we will roam.
With every heartbeat, we'll unite,
In the stillness of the night.

Woven Threads of Existence

Life's tapestry, colors blend,
Thread by thread, we start to mend.
Fates entwined in patterns bright,
Woven snugly, hearts take flight.

Each choice made, a stitch in time,
Every moment, a gentle rhyme.
In joy and sorrow, threads align,
Crafting stories, yours and mine.

Seasons change, yet we remain,
Bound by love, not cast in pain.
Through the fabric, warmth we share,
An embrace, an answered prayer.

Threads of kindness, pure and true,
Stretched across the vast and blue.
In unity, we find our place,
Woven tightly, face to face.

Together, we'll weave our fate,
In this life, we celebrate.
The loom awaits, let's intertwine,
In this dance, your heart's in mine.

The Sanctuary of Moments

Time flows gently in the sun,
Whispers of what we've begun.
In this sanctuary, we find,
Echoes soft, both rare and kind.

Every laugh, a treasure chest,
Memories that never rest.
In the stillness, joy awakes,
Born from love, the heart remakes.

Captured glances, fleeting sights,
Moments bound by gentle lights.
In still water, reflections gleam,
The sanctuary of a dream.

Time may slip like sand through hands,
Yet in this space, love understands.
Hold each second, cherish deep,
In this haven, moments keep.

Footprints etched upon the heart,
Each one plays an endless part.
In the tapestry of time,
We find solace, love's sweet chime.

Tethered to My Heartbeat

In the quiet night, whispers convene,
Silent beats echo in the unseen.
Every pulse a tether, holding me near,
An anchor of love, dispelling the fear.

Through the storm, through the night,
Your essence binds me, pure delight.
In shadows deep, your light shines clear,
Tethered to you, my heart knows no fear.

With every sigh, we weave our dreams,
In the tapestry of life, we flow like streams.
Together we dance, forever in tune,
Wrapped in the softness of a golden moon.

Time may wane, yet we will endure,
For in this bond, we find the cure.
A symphony played on heartstrings tight,
Tethered in love, we own the night.

The Dance of Belonging

In the circle of smiles, we find our way,
Hands interlocked, we refuse to sway.
With laughter that rises, we take our stand,
The dance of belonging, a joyous band.

Feet shuffling softly, we glide and spin,
In the embrace of friendship, we all begin.
Every twirl a promise, every step a thread,
Weaving together what's unsaid.

Echoes of stories, the past on our lips,
In every connection, our heart gently dips.
The rhythm of life pulls us near,
In this dance of belonging, we conquer fear.

Around the fire, melodies soar high,
In the warmth of togetherness, we touch the sky.
With every heartbeat, our spirits rise,
The dance of belonging, a sweet surprise.

Essence Lingers in Twilight

As day sheds light, dusk starts to bloom,
A gentle caress, a promise of gloom.
Whispers of secrets float on the breeze,
In twilight's embrace, the spirit finds ease.

Colors of passion paint the night sky,
The essence of moments that never say goodbye.
With every heartbeat, shadows take flight,
In the dance of silence, we greet the night.

Fading reflections in the twilight glow,
Memories linger, softly they flow.
In this serene space, we breathe as one,
Essence of twilight, our journey begun.

Stars wink above, watching our plight,
Guiding our hearts in the cool of the night.
As whispers of twilight fade into dreams,
We carry their essence, or so it seems.

Roots of My Being

Deep in the soil where silence sings,
Roots intertwine with ancient things.
Carried by whispers, the past draws me in,
Grounded in heritage, where life begins.

Each story etched in the bark of the tree,
Branches extending, embracing the free.
I stand with my roots, proud and tall,
Connected to earth, I rise, I fall.

In storms of life, I sway but hold tight,
Fierce like the thunder, soft as the light.
With every challenge, I dig in deep,
Rooted in courage, promises I keep.

Seasons may change, yet I remain,
In the harmony of life, joy and pain.
For roots of my being, unwavering embrace,
In the dance of existence, I find my place.

The Lens of Acceptance

Through the glass, I seek the truth,
A world beyond my easy view.
Acceptance blooms in vibrant hues,
A soothing balm for tender wounds.

With every glance, I learn to see,
The beauty wrapped in diversity.
In open hearts, we share the light,
Transforming shadows into bright.

Each flaw, a part of the whole we are,
A constellation, every scar.
With gentle eyes, we find our place,
In this vast web of warm embrace.

Through the lens, I find my peace,
As judgments fade and worries cease.
An inner calm begins to grow,
In acceptance, love's currents flow.

So let us cherish every soul,
Together, we become the whole.
In unity, our spirits rise,
With open hearts, we touch the skies.

The Keeper of Dreams

In the quiet of the night,
Whispers dance on silver light.
A keeper waits with tender hands,
To cradle dreams and all their strands.

Each wish a star, a glowing spark,
In the vastness, they leave their mark.
With softest eyes, they hold the hope,
Weaving fate with deftest rope.

Through shadows deep and laughter bright,
The keeper guards with all their might.
A silent promise in their gaze,
To guide us through the darkest days.

With every dawn, new dreams arise,
Like daffodils in morning's guise.
They bloom and grow, take flight and soar,
A promise of what's yet in store.

So trust the keeper, close your eyes,
For in their hands, your spirit flies.
In dreams, you'll find the path you seek,
A journey where your heart can speak.

Soliloquy of Self

In quiet corners of my mind,
I search for truths I wish to find.
A dialogue that softly flows,
Revealing layers, like a rose.

What whispers linger in the air,
Unearthed by time, a fleeting stare?
The tales I tell, both bright and dark,
Uneven paths that leave a mark.

Each thought, a thread in tapestry,
Woven tales of who I wish to be.
With every fear laid gently bare,
I spark the light, dissolve despair.

A mirror held to fractured soul,
Revealing pieces, making whole.
In words I speak, my heart takes flight,
A soliloquy that brings delight.

Embrace the journey, truth and grace,
In every silence, find your space.
For self is deep, a sacred well,
In whispers soft, our stories swell.

The Rhythm of My Heartbeat

In every thump, a song is played,
A symphony that never fades.
With every breath, I feel the beat,
The dance of life beneath my feet.

A cadence born from joy and pain,
In moments lost, and dreams in gain.
With every pulse, I find my way,
A heartbeat echoing the day.

In harmony, my spirit sings,
With every challenge, new life brings.
Through ups and downs, I learn to sway,
The rhythm guides me on my way.

With whispered notes in quiet hours,
I feel the world, its endless powers.
In sync with nature's soothing flow,
I find the strength to rise and grow.

So let me dance with heart so bold,
In every beat, a story told.
For in this rhythm, I am free,
The heartbeat of my soul's decree.

The Canvas of My Existence

On the canvas vast and wide,
Colors blend and often collide,
Each stroke a choice, a stroke of fate,
Creating art, shaping my state.

Brushes dance in morning's light,
Whispers of dreams take their flight,
With every hue, a story told,
A journey of the brave and bold.

Shadows cast from moments past,
Sunset hues that fade so fast,
Life a portrait, ever bright,
In the silence finds its might.

Textures rich in layers deep,
Secrets hidden, memories keep,
I find the beauty in each flaw,
The canvas speaks what I once saw.

In every corner, love resides,
An artist's heart where hope abides,
With every glance, I see my way,
The canvas blooms, come what may.

Echoes Beneath the Surface

In still waters, whispers hide,
Echoes drift with the rising tide,
What lies deep is seldom shown,
Secrets wrapped like seeds not sown.

Ripples dance upon my mind,
Soft reflections, truths entwined,
In silence, voices gently plead,
To uncover what souls indeed need.

Beneath the quiet, storms may brew,
Layers thick with shades of blue,
Yet also light, a glimmer's spark,
Within the shadows, fears embark.

I delve deeper to unearth,
The echoes of my worth and birth,
Each sound a part of the whole,
Mapping pathways of my soul.

In the depths, I find my song,
A melody that feels so strong,
Through the waters, I will swim,
To embrace my vision's hymn.

My Journey's Song

Footsteps echo on the trail,
Guided by the heart's soft sail,
Every step a note, a rhyme,
In the symphony of time.

Mountains rise and valleys bend,
Through each twist, I find a friend,
With the wind a whispered tune,
Chasing dreams beneath the moon.

Rhythms thrum in the night air,
Stars above, they brightly dare,
To shine a light, to show the way,
As night gives in to break of day.

With laughter, tears, and lessons learned,
Each page flipped, each memory turned,
The music flows, my spirit sings,
A melody the journey brings.

In every chord, my heart intertwines,
With destiny in perfect lines,
A song unique, forever mine,
A journey's dance, a life divine.

The Heart's Quiet Revolution

In the hush where whispers dwell,
Stirs a change, a silent swell,
The heart beats a brand new drum,
Where once was fear, now courage comes.

Tenderly, I learn to trust,
In my own strength, rise from dust,
With small revolutions, day by day,
A brighter path in shades of gray.

Vows to self, the strongest kind,
To break the chains that bind the mind,
With every breath, I stand and sing,
Of love anew and everything.

A quiet flame ignites the soul,
Transforming pieces, making whole,
No louder roar than this soft grace,
In stillness, I find my place.

As blossoms bloom from roots untold,
My heart reveals, courageous and bold,
A revolution in the heart's embrace,
A gentle shift, a sacred space.

Shelter in My Reflection

In the mirror, a glance is caught,
A face of dreams, a world sought.
Within those eyes, stories dwell,
A silent echo, a whispered spell.

Time shelters hopes behind the glass,
Fleeting moments, they swiftly pass.
Yet in the stillness, strength is found,
In every heartbeat, love unbound.

A refuge built in a fleeting gaze,
Lost in thoughts, in a gentle haze.
I find my peace in the softest light,
A tapestry woven, heart taking flight.

Each reflection a chance to see,
The depth of who I long to be.
Murmurs of wisdom softly call,
In the silence, I rise, I fall.

So I stand fast, embrace my fate,
In this sanctuary, I contemplate.
Behind those eyes, the world is vast,
In the mirror's warmth, I am home at last.

Unraveling Inner Truths

Peeling layers, one by one,
Searching for light, beneath the sun.
Whispers of secrets, softly plead,
In the quiet, I plant a seed.

Beneath the chaos, a calm resides,
Amidst the noise, my spirit hides.
Unraveling tales of joy and pain,
In tangled thoughts, there's much to gain.

Every tear, a lesson learned,
In every fire, my heart has burned.
Truths emerge from shadows deep,
In quiet moments, the soul can speak.

Embracing fears, I'm not alone,
In courage found, my heart has grown.
With open arms, I face the storm,
In vulnerability, I find my form.

I continue to dig, to seek, to find,
In every layer, a thread entwined.
Unraveling paths of the heart's pursuit,
In discovery's light, my spirit roots.

Notes in the Silence

In the hush of twilight, dreams arise,
Soft melodies beneath the skies.
Each pause a note, profound and clear,
In the silence, I draw near.

Gentle whispers of the night,
Guiding thoughts, igniting light.
Moments flutter like butterflies,
Carrying secrets, wisdoms wise.

Nature breathes in measured tones,
In solitude, the heart atones.
Every silence a story told,
In the quiet, I find the bold.

Listening deeply, I start to grow,
Feeling the warmth of an inner glow.
In tranquil spaces, my spirit sings,
Painting joy with invisible wings.

So I linger, savor the pause,
In the stillness, I find my cause.
Each note, a lifeline, softly spun,
In the music of silence, I am one.

Grasping the Present

In a fleeting moment, I stand still,
Catching the breath, the time to fill.
The present whispers, soft yet loud,
Wrapped in beauty, beneath the cloud.

With open hands, I hold today,
In the now, worries fray.
Moments shimmer like morning dew,
In every heartbeat, I start anew.

Time unfurls, a delicate thread,
Connecting dreams that lie ahead.
In the embrace of the here and now,
I find the strength, I learn to bow.

Glimmers of joy in the mundane,
In laughter, love, and gentle rain.
This present gift, so rich, so true,
In every step, I'm passing through.

So I grasp tightly, this fleeting light,
In the essence of life, darkness takes flight.
With grateful heart, I take a stand,
In the present's hold, I make my brand.

Keeping the Spirit Close

In quiet moments, whispers call,
The memories that rise and fall.
Embrace the light, a gentle glow,
Keeping the spirit close, I know.

Through every trial, every tear,
Their presence lingers ever near.
A bond that time cannot erase,
In heart and soul, they leave their trace.

With every laugh, and every sigh,
The echoes of the past float by.
In stillness, feel their warm caress,
Keeping the spirit close, I bless.

Under the stars, I pause to dream,
Knowing they're part of my stream.
In the gentle breeze, I hear their name,
Keeping the spirit close, the same.

In love's embrace, they softly shine,
Reminding me that they're still mine.
Through every heartbeat, every song,
Keeping the spirit close, I'm strong.

The Haven of Me

In the quiet of my mind's domain,
Feelings of peace gently reign.
A sanctuary where I reside,
The haven of me, where dreams abide.

Underneath the skies so wide,
I find my strength, my heart's true guide.
Here in shadows, light does play,
The haven of me, night and day.

Through every storm, the winds may wail,
Yet in this space, I shall not fail.
Reflections echo, soft and clear,
The haven of me keeps me near.

With whispers from the fading light,
I feel the warmth, I feel the fight.
In solitude, I am set free,
The haven of me, my decree.

Amidst the chaos, I find my way,
Guided by the words I say.
In gentle breaths, serenity,
The haven of me, my clarity.

Crystals of Memory

Shining brightly in the mind's eye,
Crystals of memory will not die.
Each fragment, a treasure held so dear,
Reflecting moments, laughter, and fear.

In shades of joy, in hues of pain,
Crystals of memory will remain.
Each story woven, layer by layer,
Flickering softly, a guiding prayer.

Through the corridors where shadows play,
Crystals of memory light the way.
With every glance, they tell a tale,
Of love and hope that will prevail.

In quiet spaces, they softly gleam,
Crystals of memory, like a dream.
Holding close all I cherish most,
With every heartbeat, they're my host.

In the fabric of my soul they dwell,
Crystals of memory weave their spell.
In shimmering light, I find my place,
Embracing all, I softly trace.

Guardians of My Heart

In gentle whispers, they appear,
Guardians of my heart, so near.
With loving arms, they shield the soul,
In their embrace, I feel quite whole.

Through darkest nights, their light does shine,
Guardians of my heart, divine.
With every heartbeat, every tear,
Their strength provides a silent cheer.

In moments frail, they comfort me,
Guardians of my heart, I see.
An unseen force guiding my way,
With gratitude, I pause to pray.

In laughter shared, in silence deep,
Guardians of my heart, they keep.
The essence of love in every part,
A bond that never will depart.

Through all my journeys, near and far,
Guardians of my heart, my star.
With gentle grace, they light the dark,
Forever cherished, a loving mark.

Milton Keynes UK
Ingram Content Group UK Ltd.
UKHW021857151124
451262UK00014B/1324

9 789916 791004